Timothy Hubble
and the
KING CAKE PARTY

YOU ARE INVITED TO A KING CAKE PARTY

SATURDAY, 2:00 PM

AT THE HOME OF

{ AMANDA AND ADAM LEBLANC }

RSVP

Timothy Hubble
and the
KING CAKE PARTY

By Anita C. Prieto

Illustrated by
Virginia Howard

PELICAN PUBLISHING COMPANY
GRETNA 2009

For Sarah Elizabeth and her cousins, Abigail, Luke, Jacob, Caleb, Caroline, and Kailyn, who love to eat king cake

The word "Pelican" and the depiction of a pelican are trademarks of Pelican Publishing Company, Inc., and are registered in the U.S. Patent and Trademark Office.

Library of Congress Cataloging-in-Publication Data

Prieto, Anita C., 1933-
  Timothy Hubble and the king cake party / by Anita C. Prieto ; illustrated by Virginia Howard.
      p. cm.
   Summary: Having recently moved to New Orleans, seven-year-old Timmy is worried about the invitation he received for a king cake party, a Mardi Gras tradition celebrating the three wise men's visit to the baby Jesus.
   ISBN 978-1-58980-584-2 (hardcover : alk. paper) [1. King cake--Fiction. 2. Parties--Fiction. 3. Worry--Fiction. 4. New Orleans (La.)--Fiction.] I. Howard, Virginia, ill. II. Title.
   PZ7.P9352Ti 2009
   [E]--dc22

                                      2008030469

Printed in Singapore
Published by Pelican Publishing Company, Inc.
1000 Burmaster Street, Gretna, Louisiana 70053

TIMOTHY HUBBLE AND THE KING CAKE PARTY

"Mom, I've got mail!" Seven-year-old Timothy Hubble raced into his house, almost stumbling over Blue, his beautiful Siamese cat.

"I'm invited to a king cake party," he said. "What's that?"

"I'm not sure, Timmy," his mom said. "But the invitation came from your new friend, Adam. Go ask him."

Next door, Adam LeBlanc, his twin sister, Amanda, and their mom were building a large model of a T-Rex dinosaur.

Timmy sat next to Adam. "I got your invitation," he said.

"Can you come?" Adam asked.

"I've never been to a king cake party," Timmy said. "Do I have to bring a present?"

Mrs. LeBlanc smiled. "No," she said. "You've just moved to New Orleans, Timmy, so you wouldn't know about king cake parties. We hold them from January 6—Kings' Day—to Mardi Gras Day. They remind us of the day the Magi—the three kings—arrived in Bethlehem to visit the Baby Jesus."

"It's a New Orleans custom," Adam added. "Get it?"

"I guess," Timmy said softly. But he really did not understand at all.

"King cakes—yum,"
Adam said, licking his lips. "I love the purple slices."

"A purple cake?" Timmy exclaimed, trying to picture
it. "That's different!"

"It *is* different," Amanda said. "A king cake is long—
and flat—with a hole in the middle."

The picture in Timmy's head got even more curious.

"Actually, it has purple, green, and gold icing," Adam
said. "Like Mardi Gras colors."

A long, flat cake? A hole in the middle? Purple, green,
and gold icing? Timmy's head was reeling. *And* he was
getting worried. King cake parties sounded very
strange.

"When we cut the king cake," Amanda said, "I hope I
get the baby."

"What baby?" Timmy sputtered.

"It's in the cake, silly," Amanda said. "The baby is
baked in the cake."

Timmy gulped. "A baby? Baked in the cake?"
This party sounded totally weird!

"It's a plastic baby," Amanda explained. "It
represents the Baby Jesus. If you find the baby
in your slice of cake, you'll be crowned the king."

"The king picks a queen," Adam said, "and they give the next party. But only if they want to," he added quickly.

Even though he was very confused, Timmy said, "Sounds like fun."

"So you'll come?" Adam asked. "Amanda and I get to invite three friends each."

"Girls?" Timmy cried. "There'll be girls at the party, too?"

"Yeah, but don't worry," Adam said. "They won't bother us boys."

That night, Timmy had dinner with his family—Mom, Dad, his three-year-old sister, Marie, and Grandpa. He explained what he had heard about king cakes, ending with a big sigh.

"You don't seem excited about the party," Mom said.

"I'm worried," Timmy admitted softly. "I won't know most of those kids."

"That's exactly why you *should* go," Mom said, "to meet new friends."

"Anything else bothering you, son?" Dad asked.

Timmy squirmed in his chair. "Dad," he said, "there'll be girls at that party. Yuck!"

"That wouldn't stop me," Dad said. "Girls usually ignore boys anyway."

"I guess so," Timmy agreed.

"What else?" Grandpa demanded.

"Well, Grandpa," Timmy said, "suppose I get the baby and none of those girls will be my queen? Wouldn't that be terrible?"

"I declare!" Grandpa exclaimed. "You are the biggest worrywart I know." Then Grandpa laughed. "Besides, that cake will be cut into so many pieces—what chance will you have to get that baby?"

"Not much," Timmy said, smiling.

That night, after Timmy climbed into bed, he could not fall asleep. "Now I have a new worry," he whispered to Blue, who had snuggled next to him. Suppose I go to the party and I *don't* get the baby. Wouldn't that be terrible, Blue? My first king cake party and I don't get the little plastic baby."

Timmy sighed and turned over on his pillow.
"Grandpa's right. I guess I *am* the biggest
worrywart in town," he mumbled as his eyes
closed and he fell asleep.

Saturday was a beautiful winter day—perfect
for a king cake party.

When Timmy arrived at the party, he met Adam's friends, Taylor and Logan. Amanda introduced him to Abigail, Casey, and Marie. Just as Dad had predicted, the girls went upstairs to play, while the boys played soccer outside.

Later, everyone came together in the den, where Timmy found himself sitting next to Marie.

"My little sister's name is Marie," he said shyly.

"Is she that cute little girl with brown curls that I've seen you playing with in your yard?" Marie asked.

Timmy grinned. "Yeah," he said, "that's Marie." Suddenly, Timmy realized that Marie, Abigail, and Casey were not strange at all. They had become part of his new circle of friends. *I guess I worried about that for nothing*, he thought, smiling.

"Time for king cake," Mrs. LeBlanc called.

Everyone watched as Mr. LeBlanc brought in the king cake. The mouth-watering treat smelled of cinnamon and sugar. Timmy thought he had never smelled anything so delicious in all his life.

Mrs. LeBlanc passed around mugs of hot chocolate topped with marshmallow creme, saying, "Be careful. It's hot."

But no one was listening. Every eye was on Mr. LeBlanc, who was carefully slicing the king cake into ten large pieces.

And then it was time to choose.

Marie leaned over and whispered to Timmy, "I always poke around in my piece before I bite into it, to see if the baby's inside."

"Good idea," Timmy said.

"We'll let Timmy pick first," Adam announced, "because it's his first king cake party."

It was so hard to choose. Timmy could not make up his mind. Should he choose this gold slice? Maybe the baby was in that green piece. Timmy really wanted that baby. He made a wish and chose a big purple slice of king cake.

"Let's wait until everyone has picked," Mrs. LeBlanc said. "Then we'll bite into our slices together."

Soon everyone had chosen a piece of king cake.
The time had come.

Who would find the baby?

The eight friends looked at each other, giggling.

Marie poked at her slice. Timmy poked at his,
too. So did all the others.

Suddenly, Abigail cried out, "I've got the baby!
I feel it under my finger."

Timmy's heart sank.

But before Timmy could feel too disappointed,
Logan yelled, "Me, too! I've got the baby, too!"

Then everyone was shouting, "Me, too! Me, too!"

Everyone had found the baby!

Mr. and Mrs. LeBlanc laughed. "We wanted Timmy's
first king cake party to be special," they explained. "So
the baker made sure *everyone* got a baby."

"And crowns for everyone, too?" Adam asked.

"Absolutely!" Mr. LeBlanc said.

That evening, Timmy could not stop talking about the party. He wore his crown until it was time for bed.

"I made a lot of new friends today," he told his
mom as they climbed the stairs that night.

In his bedroom, Timmy hung his crown on the bedpost. He sat the plastic baby on the night-stand and climbed into bed, followed by Blue. Snuggled under the covers, he thought about the party.

"Sometimes it's really silly to worry about what's going to happen," he whispered to Blue. "Sometimes it's better just to wait and see."

Timmy yawned and took one last look at the tiny plastic baby. "Tomorrow," he mumbled just before he fell asleep, "tomorrow I'm going to ask Mom and Dad if I can have a king cake party at our house next weekend."

Easy King Cake Recipe

To make a delicious king cake for your own party, you will need:

1 can (17.5 oz.) large cinnamon rolls with icing
Purple, green, and gold (yellow) sugar crystals
Large cookie sheet (11" x 17") covered with nonstick aluminum foil
Small plastic baby or large dried bean to represent Baby Jesus

Open the can of rolls. Uncoil each roll into a long strip of dough.

Braid two strips of dough together. Do the same with two more strips. Fold the last strip of dough in half and braid the two halves together.

Arrange the three braided strips on the cookie sheet so that they form an oval. Pinch the ends of the strips together to secure the oval. With an adult's help, bake according to instructions on the cinnamon roll can.

When the cake is done, remove it from the oven, cover it with icing, and immediately sprinkle colored sugars in 2-inch-wide strips of purple, green, and gold. Once the cake has cooled, hide the plastic baby under a piece of cake.

Call your friends and invite them to your king cake party! Bon Appetit!

Note: You can probably find the plastic baby and colored sugar crystals at a party supply shop. You can also make your own colored sugar by mixing in a plastic bag 1 or 2 drops of food coloring with ½ cup of granulated sugar.